ESCAPE FROM CHILD SEXUAL ABUSE

HANDBOOK OF SEX EDUCATION THAT IS *VALUE BASED* *AGE APPROPRIATE* *CULTURE SPECIFIC*

S SHARMILA

<u>*Dedication*</u>

To My Sons, Vijendraa & Sivendraa..

Im writing this book to get my sons generation & future generation grow into healthy, loving, trustworthy, compassionate and sexually conscious adults...

<u>**Thanks**</u>

To the two who gave me life

&

To the one who made me realize, who I am!!!

Contents

Preface

Child sexual abuse!!! A new but familiar topic nowadays...

I was surprised to notice atleast one news about child sexual abuse in any corner of the country. One such news that hit my mind was, a kindergarden kid was abused by bus driver. It was running in my mind for around 2 weeks, I was searching what I can do to protect kids from abusers!!! Finally, I decided to do a deep study on child sexual abuse and completed certification courses to become a child sexuality educator.

Kids are able to protect themselves against sexual abuse... Then why aren't we teaching them, How to?

This book helps in making the kid understand taboo topics clearly with fun filled explanations & activities. So they can be the Little Ambassadors For Child Sexuality Literacy.

ACKNOWLEDGEMENTS

I truly have no idea where I'd be, if he hadn't given me a roof over my head or took the role of a mother to my kids in my absence. My hearty thankful to my husband, Satha and to my family members.

Writing a book is harder than I thought... None of this would have been possible without my sister, Pooja who was my moral support, advisor of Vidhay, editor of this book. We both read this book 50+ times to add some hot and spicy to the content.

A very special thanks to my editor of this book and content writer of Vidhay, Aruna who gave life to my dream of writing a book. When I conveyed my wish of writing a book on child sexual abuse, she was the one who said, no worries Sharmi, I'm there to help you out. And she did it.

I
Introduction

Shhhhh...... Close your eyes!!! says Amma, Go bring some water says Appa, immediately after seeing a kiss scene or first night scene on TV... Are they bad at watching TV? Absolutely yes!! Then who will discuss with you when you are eagerly ready to do research about taboo topics (Sex)... Appa?? Amma?? No never, because we live in a society where taboo topics are censored & left to the choice of kids to learn.. Have you ever wondered, what's inside the boy's bathroom? What's inside the girl's bathroom? What happens on the first night? Have you discussed all these with anyone? At a certain age you might feel the need of want to know more about the concept of sex. Even though sex information is available everywhere through the internet, you need proper guidance instead of misleading media and magazines. When you grow up you need to adapt to the changes that occur in different stages of your development. Girls are afraid, why is my breast paining at this young age? Boys feel why am I wet in my dreams? This is common at a certain point of age.

Statistics about child sexual abuse

The need for sex education is to provide you with the right concept on sex and the changes that take place in your body as you age. In our society, it is very important that you learn, at the right age, about sex and other terms that are associated with it. As a child you should be aware of the term 'consent' and understand its meaning and importance. Sex education also teaches you to respect others' right to their body, the changes that happen in your body, and in maintaining healthy relationships with others. With the right awareness on sex, you will not only understand the process of puberty and body changes but also get a full understanding of your body and opposite gender and most importantly how to say 'no' to any unwanted sexual activities. This leads to the strong basement in reducing or stopping child sexual abuse, facing it boldly & to come out of it. This also builds self confidence in kids.

Glimpse Of Child Sexual Abuse

Any harm or mistreatment to a child is considered to be abuse. Ok then, if your uncle hits you, is it an abuse? Obviously yes... If someone (it can be anyone) hits you rudely it is an abuse... Now it's time to explore different types of abuse,

- Physical Abuse - eg: Hitting, slapping, punching, kicking etc
- Emotional Abuse - eg: Shaming, blaming etc
- Sexual Abuse - any sexual behavior performed without a partner's consent

Child sexual abuse is an act of abuse where an adult or any other adolescent forces a child into sexual submission. This includes when someone has sexual activities with a child, indecent exposure of the genitals, etc. There are different types of child sexual abuse and they can be with contact or without contact.

- In contact abuse, the abuser would make physical contact with the child. Even touching private parts of a child without consent, is a form of child sexual abuse.
- Without contact abuse involves encouraging a child to hear about or watch sexual activities, online abuse, showing pornography to a child, etc.

In order to prevent child sexual abuse, as a kid you should be clear on what it involves. From the above you will understand some of that. Whatever form of child sexual abuse takes place, it usually ends with damaging the child both physically and mentally.

Pre Evaluation Test _ It's time to self evaluate your knowledge about sexuality with simple questions as follows. Let's begin,

1. What is the most important event for a girl when she reaches puberty?

    1. She gets taller and her breasts begin to develop.
    2. Hair grows under her arms and around her genitals.
    3. She has her first period.

2. What is the most important event for a boy when he reaches puberty?

    1. His voice gets deeper.
    2. He first ejaculates semen from his penis.
    3. He grows hair under his arms and around his genitals.

3. It is normal for a man's penis to become erect (hard):

    1. Several times a day, including in his sleep.
    2. Only when he has sexual intercourse with his wife.
    3. About once a month.

4. When a man ejaculates how many sperms are present in the semen that comes out of his penis?

    1. 1,000
    2. 300,000,000
    3. 1

5. Which three items would be good advice for a friend who is being sexually abused?

1. Tell the abuser to STOP it and do everything you can to get away.
2. Allow the sexual abuse to continue; it won't hurt you.
3. Report the abuser to a parent or another grown-up who can stop it.
4. Keep it a secret; don't tell anyone.
5. Get counseling so you can talk about your feelings about being abused.

II
Relationship

What Is Friendship?

Friends are the family you choose!!! Racing your bicycles with your friends, jumping into puddles when it rains, hiding yourselves and waiting for your friend to catch you out, and run wildly about are some of the everyday activities we do with our friends. In simple words, friendship is a state of bond where two or more individuals trust, cooperate, and share secrets between themselves. You can be friends with any person who you think resembles your character. Making friends is an important skill in life. Having a good friend along will always make you happy. You can develop friendships within your family, neighborhood, school, or even in another city. A good friendship is one where both the people involved are committed to their friendship and have a mutual sense of trust. They like to spend time together, have fun with each other, help out one other when they have a problem or are sad, and remember important things about each other. Having a friend will help you confide anything that bothers you and also find comfort in them.

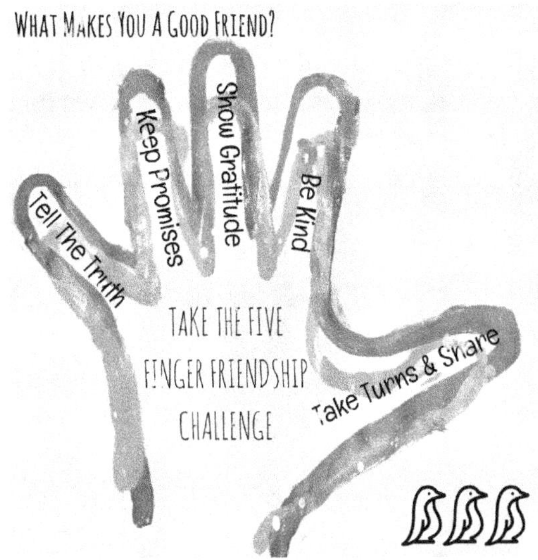

Characteristics Of A Good Friend

Characteristics Of A Friend:

It all starts when you start your walk around the neighborhood and look at kids of your age playing together. We would want to go play with them, get to know them immediately and join in the fun. But how do we choose who would actually become our friends and gain our trust? There are some characteristics you have to look out for in a friend,

- You choose your friend, firstly, by the common values you both share.
- Most often we can get the feeling that the very friend we choose keeps bullying us. But we give excuses on that front. This should not be the case. A friend is one who should stand up for you, not become the bully. There should always be a give and take in any relationship, especially friendship.

- Both you and your friend should be responsible for taking any decision.
- Among all characteristics of a good friend, comes loyalty. This is the most important part as it lets us know how much our friend will stick up for us when we need them.
- Best of all, a friend should be generous, honest and humble.

Characteristics Of Healthy Vs Unhealthy Relationships

A healthy relationship will never require you to sacrifice your friends,

Your dreams or your dignity.

- Dinkar Kalotra

I'm familiar with the term relationship, but what is a healthy / unhealthy relationship? How to differentiate it? It is very important that at your age you understand what healthy and unhealthy relationships are. We often step into the world without any idea as to what having a good relationship feels like. Here, you can learn about the characteristics of both healthy and an unhealthy relationship.

Healthy relationship:

Respecting both yourself and others involved in the relationship. It is where all members included are free to grow and live in harmony with each other.

- **Equality** – Both parties of the relationship treat the other as an equal.
- **Respect** – Both members value and respect each other's dignity.
- **Communication** – Feeling comfortable when you express your opinions and ideas to each other.
- **Support** – Encouraging each other in their dreams and goals.

- **Non-threatening behaviour** – Feeling safe in the relationship and not worrying that the other person might harm you.

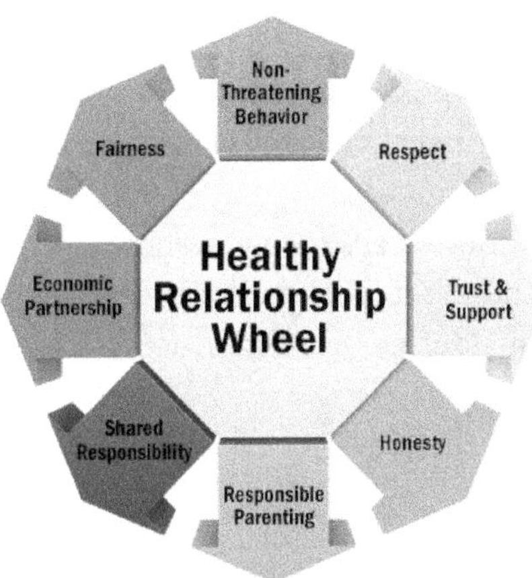

Healthy Relationship Wheel

Unhealthy relationship:

Here, one member tries to grow or gain better by undermining, controlling, abusing or exerting power over the other person.

- **Manipulation** – It is of many forms and can include convincing the other person to ignore their needs, wants and desires.
- **Jealousy** – A jealous relationship is unhealthy when it is constant and excessive.
- **Criticism** – Criticizing the other person and trying to bring them down emotionally.
- **Fighting** – This could prove to be a bad sign in the relationship.
- **Controlling behaviour** – It includes controlling where others go, see, do and speak. Any sort of emotional, physical and verbal abuse is also another form of controlling.

Activity:

Circle the healthy relationship from the following:

1. An adult person whom you trust shows you pornography
2. An adult person helps you out when you are feeling confused with your situation
3. Someone you know keeps trying to show you nude pictures.
4. Someone on the street is always following you constantly.
5. A friend or an elder person listens to you and helps you when you are in a dilemma.
6. When you are feeling low, your friend or an elder person tries to cheer you up.

Social Media Influence To Kids:

Like, Share, Comment!!! I bet you know what these terms are! But how? Is this in your syllabus? Nobody taught you about these terms. How did you become familiar with them? How have they affected your life?

Questions like these are often something we forget to ask ourselves. Rather than playing outside, chit chat with friends, writing letters to friends, sending them greeting cards, everything has changed as time flies. Instead, Facebook communities, whatsapp chats, sending emojis, Gif files for wishes and spending time on a Smartphone has become your way of relaxing after a day at school. But is social media healthy for you?

Many social media want their users to be more than 13 years old. But in a recent survey of parents, it was shocking to know the average age of kids using social media are 7 to 12 years. It is time you got to know whether you are being safe on social media. Let's see the positive & negative sides of it.

Positive effects:

- Spending time online at your age to pick up some necessary skill set.
- Social media interaction is also a way of interacting with the world and knowing what the current trends are.
- With such a presence, you will be able to maintain long-term friendships.

Negative effects:

- One important downside of social media is the addiction it causes. When you get addicted to social media, you end up spending hours, every day, in it. This affects your daily normal routine.
- Creates poor mental health in kids.
- Obsession to always staying online by posting pictures, updates and posts increases narcissism (too much self-interest in oneself).
- Cyber bullying.

Coming to the changes in daily behaviour at home like:

- Increased irritability
- Increased anxiety
- Lack of self-esteem.

Know the importance of social media on the positive side, utilize it and never let social media to rule you.

III
About Our Body

"Adults / as kids, you may have layer upon layer in your minds on stuff that are related to sex and sexuality, and it is the responsibility of the trusted person to strip back those layers."

It was a period where our elders felt their own shame, fear and guilt which keeps them in the dark. It is now time to change the way we think, As we are the next generation of children. Naming body parts correctly is a great start to ensure that you are open for communication with parents or grown-ups about sex and sexuality. If you have started with these conversations at a very early age, you will feel more comfortable speaking out and ask any queries you might have. If you are under the age of 5, then a good place to start talking about body parts is during your bath time.

You need to be taught about eyes, nose, ears, elbows, shoulders, vulva, penis, scrotum and vagina, all in the same tone while introducing the concept of private parts by explaining that genital regions, nipples and mouths are "just for you". It's OK to touch your private body parts but, remember, private parts are just for you. We don't do that in front of other people and don't let others touch / see without our consent. It is yours & "just for you".

Genital Body Parts And Its Functions:

At some point, you might have wondered about what the genital body parts are and their uses. Let us explain it to you.

Genital parts are basic body parts that differentiate the male from the female gender. These parts also have some functions to perform and are usually called private parts since they are always covered by the clothes we wear.

If you wish to talk to someone about your private parts, you can always talk to your mom or dad about them, privately, in your house. Avoid talking about these in public. Some of the body parts and their functions of the male and the female are given here.

Male genital body parts:

- **Scrotum:** It is a pouch-like structure that is responsible for holding the testicles and many nerves and blood vessels and is situated behind the penis.
- **Penis:** The penis is the male reproductive organ that allows sexual intercourse to take place. The layer of the penis will be loose and elastic, for changing its size during an erection. Semen, that carries sperm, will be expelled (ejaculated) through penis when a he attains sexual climax (orgasm).
- **Testicles:** Testicles are organs that are found in pairs in the scrotum. They are responsible for producing sperms which are necessary for reproduction.

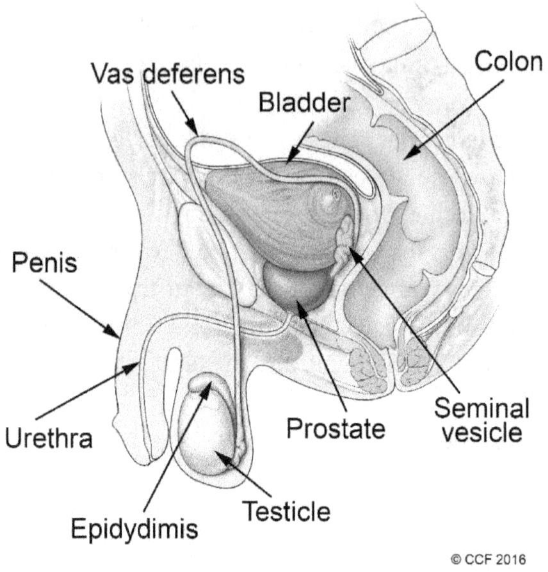

Male genital body part

Female genital body parts:

It perform teamwork in enabling reproduction, pregnancy, and childbirth.

- **Ovaries**: Females have 2 ovaries and perform key functions, producing hormones and releasing eggs.
- **Fallopian tubes:** Acts as passage to carry eggs.
- **Uterus / Womb:** After ovulation, if an egg is not fertilized, the egg dies, ruptures and comes out as blood, it leaves through the vagina. The process is called menstruation / periods. If an egg is fertilized by sperm, the cells divide and grow, becoming an embryo.

- **Cervix:** Narrow structure at the bottom of the uterus, functions are Producing mucus, Protecting against bacteria, Allowing fluids to drain.
- **Vagina:** The vagina is a flexible structure that connects the woman's internal and external reproductive organs. It lies below the cervix, allows menstrual blood to leave the body and is responsible for allowing the semen to flow during intercourse.
- **Clitoris:** This organ lies above the vagina, responsible for sexual stimulation and is a sensitive part of the female genital.
- **Vulva:** The vulva includes all the external parts of the female reproductive system like the hymen, vestibule, urethra, etc.

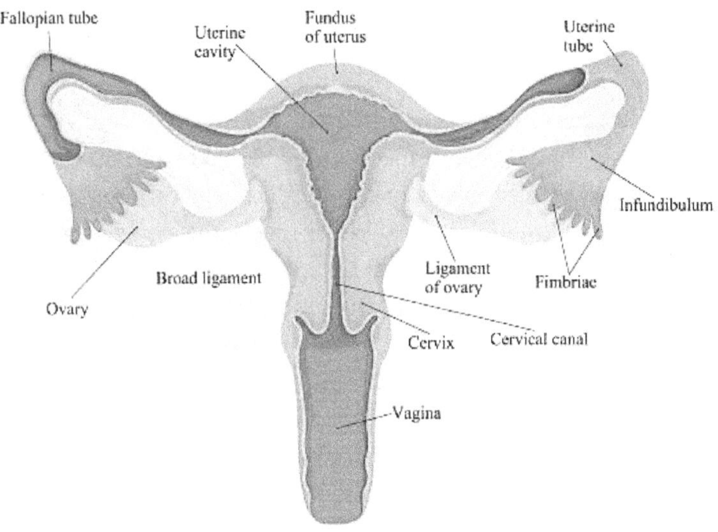

Female genital body part

Now you know the basic private parts of human anatomy. Always seek the help of your parents or some other elders you trust if you feel that your private parts are being abused in any way by others.

IV
Safe Touch & Unsafe Touch

Whenever mummy gives me a hug and kiss at night, it always feels good. Every time daddy comes home and takes me up in the air with hugs and kisses always feels good. But I feel different when my uncle hugs me, when my aunty kisses me? Same thing is happening but why am I feeling different? Let's learn the reason behind this. It's time to introduce safe & unsafe touch / behaviour

- Safe behavior / Good touch: It makes someone feel positive and keeps them in their comfort zone. And remember whatever happens in the presence of your parents, it is a safe touch. Eg: A handshake, a pat on the head, mother's hug.
- Unsafe behavior / Bad touch: It makes a person feel insecure and uncomfortable. It affects the person both mentally and physically. Eg: Hitting, touching private parts, pinching, etc.

If you don't want or don't feel comfortable with any sort of touch or behaviour from a person or at that moment, you can always say 'NO' even if it is from a familiar or unfamiliar person or someone whom you know for a long time. By doing so you set your personal boundaries and refrain from any further uneasiness.

Unsafe Touch

Activity:

Identify good touch & bad touch from the given situations:

- A mother giving a hug to her child when he comes home from school.
- Someone touches a child and tells him/her not to tell anyone.
- A stranger touching your private parts.
- Getting a pat from the teacher.
- Brother pulling your cheeks.
- Someone trying to hurt or threaten you.
- Grandmother giving a child kisses.
- A doctor examining a child in the presence of parents.

V

Gender

At this age, you are still learning the rules of the world. You can understand concepts and are interested in discussing them with a friendly person. Ideas on what gender is, can be found everywhere around you. You start by differentiating gender ever since you start to say 'mommy' and 'daddy'. Our society also tells us how boys and girls are supposed to speak, look, dress and act. You will find many people have many beliefs when it comes to gender stereotyping.

But actually, gender is something that we feel about ourself, sexuality is who we are, emotionally, physically, romantically, or sexually attracted to. Therefore, gender is something how we feel about ourselves while sexuality is how we feel about others.

Different Types Of Gender:

You can easily identify or come across two types of gender (Binary mode) in your day-to-day life i.e. the Masculine gender and the Feminine gender. But there is a spectrum of genders than the ones that meet our eyes.

Types of gender includes,

- **Masculine** - This gender denotes a male subtype. Eg: man, boy, bull, father, king, etc.

- **Feminine** - This gender denotes the female subtype. Eg: woman, girl, hen, mother, cow, etc.
- **Transgender** - Transgender people usually have their gender identity different from the gender they were thought to be at during birth.
- **Non-binary** - For people who are of non-binary gender, do not identify themselves with either the masculine or feminine gender. Because there is a very rare gender-neutral society, we should always try to acknowledge their presence too.

Once you identify the different types of gender, it becomes easier for you to acknowledge their presence and respect them equally.

Gender Identity & Equality:

Gender refers to socially constructed behaviour, roles, attributes and activities that a society considers appropriate for women, men, boys and girls and the relationships that co-exist between them.

Gender equality can be made simple as men, women, boys, girls and people of other gender, all enjoy the same opportunities, rights and protection.

Every person gets affected when gender inequality happens. It has a deep impact on people of all backgrounds and ages. Gender equality is a very important topic that you should learn at a very young age and once you have the right information, it doesn't pose a challenge. If you have any doubts you can ask any elder person who is well aware of the society norms for help.

Ways To Treat People Of All Gender With Equality And Respect:

When we start treating the people of all genders with respect and dignity, we pave the way for a society that can thrive in harmony. Some ways by which we can treat members of all gender with equality & respect include the following.

- Communicate openly and thoughtfully with all people
- Be considerate of the many opinions and views each person has which are different from your own.
- Treat everyone with consideration and respect.
- Be mindful and respectful when you wish to critique the ideas of others.
- Always be mindful of your surroundings.
- Alert any law & order personnel if you find anyone in distress or danger.
- Respect the policies and rules of all venues and meetings you go to where you can come across people of all gender types.

These are a list of some basic steps you can follow and make sure that you do not hurt or demotivate people of other gender in any way.

Activity:

True or False:

1. Men should only work in their offices while women should do only household work.
2. Women must not do certain types of work when they are pregnant.
3. Women are emotionally more considerate than men.
4. Boys should play with trucks while girls should play with dolls.
5. Men should not do kitchen work.
6. Women can become successful even in a man's career.

VI
Reproduction & STD

Reena spots blood stains in her panties!! Arun got wet during his bed time!! They were scared, because this is something unusual from their daily life? Here comes the answer. Puberty... everyone comes across this stage at some point of time. Normally, puberty starts in boys & girls when they're between 8 and 14 years old.

Girls might wonder whether boys also get periods. Kids should know these things about puberty. Girls should learn about the changes boys go through and boys should learn about those affecting girls.

- Girls breasts will begin to enlarge.
- Girls and boys get pubic hair in some places where it has never grown before, especially in private parts.
- Both girls and boys often get acne popping out in their face, sweating for no reason.
- Boys penis and testicles grow larger.
- Voice changes can be identified for boys.
- Boys sometimes have wet dreams, which means they ejaculate in their sleep.

- Girl's periods last 3 days to a week.

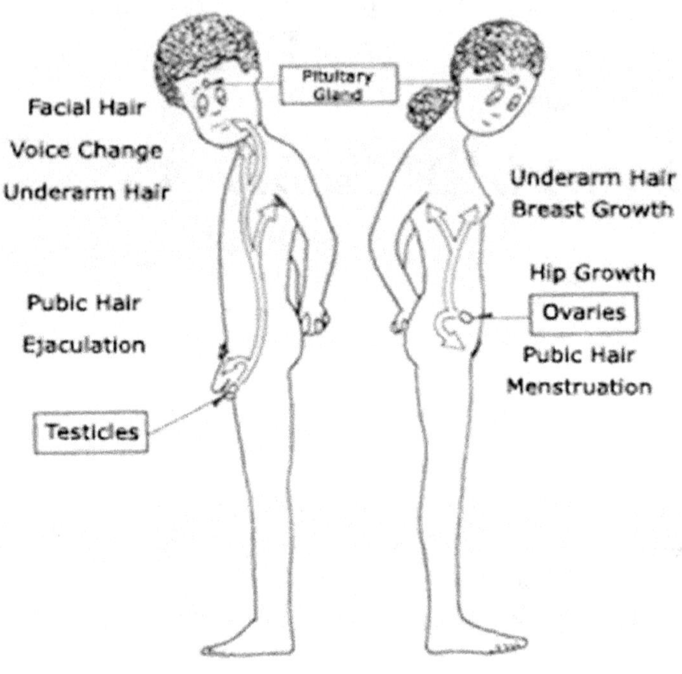

Puberty changes in both the genders

Puberty can cause all kinds of changes in your body, both physically and mentally. During this confusing time, it is important to maintain good hygiene by washing your hands, covering your mouth when sneezing or coughing, cleaning your body and teeth twice a day, washing your hands after using the toilet and before eating has proven to get rid of unwanted germs from our body. During puberty, sweat glands start acting and produce body odour which will be easily averted by washing and changing clothes regularly and bathing. Girls need to be aware of how their periods work, how often to change pad/tampon/underwear or how to dispose and clean hygienically. It's good and hygienic to change pads every 2-3 hrs, to avoid irritation & allergy.

By following some of these steps, you can maintain a healthy personal hygiene before and after puberty.

What Is Reproduction & Pregnancy In Humans?

You might have often asked the question, "Where did I come from before I was born?" This has been a question for most of us in our childhood. It is now time to learn the answer to this question. The answer lies in the process of human reproduction. Children of your age are usually curious about reproduction and pregnancy. You should understand that both reproduction and pregnancy are a normal part of our life.

For reproduction both male and female reproductive systems are needed. Lets see the 3 steps to reproduction,

- **Conception:** The male reproductive system produces the sperm and the female produces the egg cells. Semen which carries hundreds of sperm cells is ejaculated into the fallopian tube during intercourse. This then fertilizes the ovum. Note that only one sperm usually makes all the way to the ovum and forms a zygote which becomes the fetus (unborn child).
- **Pregnancy:** This stage is where the fetus starts growing inside the womb for nine months. It is connected to the mother by the umbilical cord and continues to grow its organs. During this time, the baby gets all its nutrition from the mother. The mother also undergoes a lot of changes. For eg: the tummy begins to grow bigger and bigger.
- **Childbirth:** Childbirth occurs when the fetus is fully grown inside the mother and has no more space for staying inside. The water bag in the uterus breaks and thus, starts the process of childbirth during which the baby comes out of the mother through the vagina. A baby comes out with its head first after being followed by the rest of its body. Later the umbilical cord is cut and that scar is left and remains in our body as the belly

button.

We humans pass on some of our characteristics to the offspring through genes. The genes which parents pass along to their children make them similar to the other members in the family and also make the child unique. These genes come from the male sperm and female ovum.

Let Us Recall The Human Reproductive System:

It's time for us to recall the shy topic, discussed in our biology class, nothing but the reproductive system. In humans, there are two different reproductive systems based on gender.

- A male reproductive system has two external organs (penis and scrotum) and four internal organs (accessory glands, epididymis, testes and vas deferens). A simple workflow of the male reproductive system is the testes produce sperm, which mature in the epididymis, during arousal sperm travel through the vas deferens, sperm is mixed with fluids from the accessory glands prior to ejaculation (expelling semen from the penis).
- A female reproductive system has multiple external organs (vulva) and four internal organs (Fallopian tubes, ovaries, uterus and vagina). A simple workflow of the female reproductive system is an egg is released from an ovary every month, it travels down the Fallopian tube and if sperm is present could be fertilized, that egg then travels down into the uterus where it implants and a baby is grown.
- Conception, also called fertilization, is the moment an egg and sperm fuse together to create a zygote. Birth control methods, like condoms or an IUD device are used to prevent conception (egg fertilization).

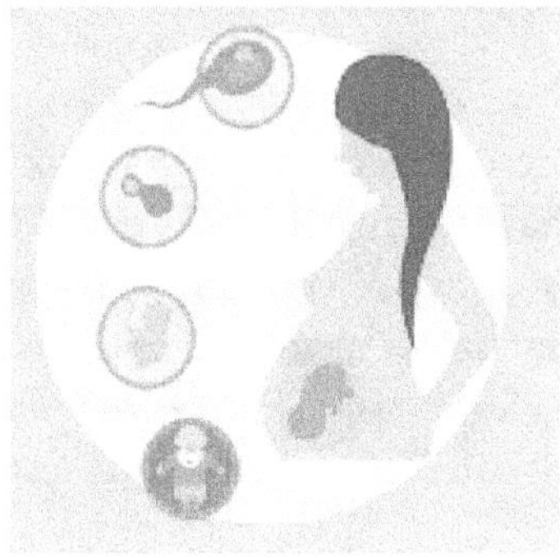

Process of pregnancy

Sexually transmitted infections (STIs) are transmitted between two humans during sex. Only four sexually transmitted infections can be cured, and they are syphilis, gonorrhea, chlamydia and trichomoniasis. Several sexually transmitted infections can be deadly if not treated, like syphilis, HIV and hepatitis B. A person can have a sexual transmitted infection without any symptoms and still transmit it to a sexual partner. The only way to be sure you or another person doesn't have a sexual transmitted infection is to get tested.

What Is Consent?

Mummy: Jim, let's ask your brother if you would like a goodbye hug.
Jim: No.
Here you can see that Jim has not given his consent to touch him. Body parts and privacy is the foundation for introducing your child to consent. To put simply, consent is a permission or agreement to let something happen. It always requires communication and respect. When you learn about consent at an early age, it will help you build better relationships with friends, family, peers and partners.

When it comes to your consent, there are some things you should know first.

- You should understand that you own your body and it belongs to you. You alone have the right to make decisions about your body.
- You can always decide if you like being hugged or kissed or touched from any family member or friends or acquaintances.
- You should also pay attention and respect other people's consent about personal boundaries. Speak up if something doesn't feel right.
- Ask for consent before you do something.
- Practice what you can do if you are in a situation where you don't feel comfortable.

Different Ways Pregnancy Can Occur:

How did your younger brother or sister get inside your mommy's stomach? You would have had many sleepless nights wondering about it. Your mom got pregnant either naturally or with some external help. Now we shall learn the different ways to conceive a child and get pregnant.

- Intrauterine insemination: This process is simple without any hassle for the woman. Here the sperm is matched with the egg inside the uterus thus, forming the zygote.
- The Turkey Baster method: This is a process where sperm is gathered from a known donor or a sperm bank and then implanting it inside the woman.
- In Vitro Fertilization (IVF): This is the process to which couples go to as the last option. Here the doctor prescribes medicines to stimulate the formation of eggs. Later these eggs are collected and fused with the sperm to form an embryo and then placed inside the uterus of the woman.

- Surrogacy: This method is usually growing a baby in someone else's womb who is called the surrogate. It is simply called renting a womb. The IVF method is used to place the embryo into the surrogate's womb. Here, the surrogate carries the baby in the womb for nine months before delivering the baby to the parents.

Different Types Of Pregnancy:

Different types of pregnancy? Who'd have thought?! Isn't there only one? The normal kind of pregnancy?

Well, yes, there is. And no, we've got many different types of pregnancy. Read on to know more about them.

- Molar pregnancy: In this type, the placenta and the embryo develop abnormally where the tissue in the placenta may become a tumor. This requires close follow-up with the doctor who removes the tissues from the uterus.
- Tubal pregnancy: This type can be dangerous to the mother. That is because the fertilized egg gets implanted somewhere else instead of the uterus, mostly in the fallopian tube.
- Singlet pregnancy: In this type, a single egg is fertilized by a single sperm thus, developing a single fetus.
- Multiple pregnancy: Here, two or more embryos are formed in the uterus and thus, creating more than one child.

My, my! There are just so many types of pregnancies? Did you know that so many types can occur? Well, read on or talk to someone if you have doubts about them.

STD & HIV:

Let us now come to the part of STD and HIV. You would have probably heard about AIDS (Acquired Immuno Deficiency

Syndrome) sometime in your life. Now we will see what causes it and how.

What is STD?

STD means Sexually Transmitted Disease, also called as Sexually Transmitted Infections (STIs). It is an infection that spreads from one person to another through intercourse. The symptoms caused by STD vary from person to person and not everyone affected will experience the same symptoms. Also, in some cases STD may not even show any symptoms.

STD that is caused by a parasite or bacteria can be cured with medication. There is no known cure for STD caused by the virus, but treatment can be taken to keep STD under control. Without treatment it can rise up to the risk of AIDS.

Some types of habits that cause STD are,

- Having sex with a number of partners
- Having sex under the influence of alcohol or drugs
- Having unprotected sex i.e. sex without using condoms.

What is HIV?

HIV is a sexually transmitted infection which leads to AIDS when left untreated. We can prevent transmission of HIV by Taking HIV medications regularly, Treatment with HIV medicines help the patient live longer and healthier lives.

Common Myths About Transmission:

So much wrong information is being passed around about STDs. You need to stay informed about the disease and learn what's true and not true. Here are some myths associated with STD.

- **Only bad people get STD.**

- STD does not discriminate between people. It affects all: the rich, poor, athletes, professors, geeks, etc. Even some people having sex for the first time can get STD.

- **If someone has STD, you can see it.**

  - STD cannot be seen. Even doctors cannot know by looking at someone if they have STD or not. One has to take tests like blood and urine samples to know for certain. A person can always get checked for STD and make sure they don't have it.

- **If you have an STD once, you cannot get it again.**

  - Some STDs can be treated. But you can get it again if you have sexual activity with someone who is infected. You can use condoms or get checked regularly with a doctor.

- **Only one partner needs to get checked before having sex. Both involved in sexual activity need not get checked.**

  - Mostly getting tested with a partner is safer for both parties involved in the intercourse to make sure that neither of them has STD.

- **You can avoid STDs by having oral sex.**

  - No!! Where there's sex there is STDs, it is better to avoid sex in any form oral, anal, vaginal to stay safe.

- **You can get an STD from a Toilet.**

  - Toilet seats are not the culprits!!

VII
Child Sexual Abuse

It is common to feel uncomfortable when someone talks to you about sexual abuse. Don't worry. It is a natural thing to feel. But talking about it will keep you safe from harm.

Most kids do not even know that they are being abused when sexual abuse happens to them. It happens across all races, religion, at all cultural lines and education levels. But 95% of the time, it is preventable through awareness.

Child Sexual Abuse

Child sexual abuse does not need to include physical contact between the child and the abuser at all times. Some forms of child sexual abuse includes,

- Fondling
- Exhibiting oneself to a minor
- Intercourse
- Sex trafficking
- Masturbating in front of a child or forcing the child to do so
- Showing obscene images or videos

Impacts:

When a child is abused, most often they are tricked or forced into sexual activities. They might not even understand that what's happening to them is wrong or that it's a form of sexual abuse. They would feel uncomfortable but would be afraid to tell someone about it. Sexual abuse can happen at any place and

any time, even in online. What is important is that it is never the child's fault and they need to understand it.

Let us see what effects child sexual abuse has on a child. The following are how sexual abuse impacts a child both mentally and physically. They can be long term or short term effects.

- Traumatic stress
- Anxiety & depression
- Suicidal thoughts
- Pregnancy
- Feeling shame and guilty
- Sexually transmitted infections
- Eating disorders
- Relationship problems with friends, family and colleagues

Experiencing sexual abuse can affect how a child thinks and feels for a lifetime, thus affecting kids' future on a whole.

Victims Know Their Abusers

Identifying Situations That May Be Uncomfortable Or Dangerous:

Knowing that someone has been sexually abused or is being abused is a difficult task. But there are some signs you can detect from them through which you can extend your help. Some signs include both physical and emotional which are listed here.

Emotional signs:

- Frightened to be alone
- Avoiding to be around people or person they know
- Alcohol or drug misuse
- Having nightmares
- Changes in eating habits
- Self harm
- Change in their mood, feeling angry, or anything contrary to their nature

Physical signs:

- Pregnancy
- Bruises
- Sexually transmitted infection
- Bleeding, pain or discharge at the genital area

Steps A Person Can Take When They Are Being Or Have Been Sexually Abused:

It is a traumatic experience to be sexually abused. To take any step in making it right, makes the person feel like they are being exposed. But what most people fail to see is that it is the abuser who should feel ashamed and not the victim. It may take victims years to speak about their experience since opening up is one of the hardest things to do.

Hearing about or reading about someone's experience also brings back all those feelings of vulnerability. But talking to someone we trust is the first step we can take in recovering. If a child or any of your friend reports being sexually abused, you should:

- Tell them it's not their fault
- Listen carefully to their story
- Make them know that they have done the right thing by speaking out
- Tell them what you'll do next
- Report what they told you as soon as possible

Even though the physical wound of a sexual assault heals, the mental impact will linger for a longer period of time. So it is important to take time to understand them and help them.

What can you say to make them feel better? Try saying the following to make the person feel better.

- It was not your fault
- I am sorry this happened to you

- You have been very brave through all this
- What will make you feel better? How can I help?

Kids Self-Protection:

Did you know that you can protect yourself from sexual abuse just by following some simple steps? Some of the ways you can protect yourself are listed here.

- Always be aware of your surroundings and do not let your guard down.
- Trust your intuition or gut feel at all times.
- Make a habit of watching out for warning signs and remove yourselves from the situation or place.
- If you feel someone is following you, immediately run to a crowded place and if possible, shout and gain attention.
- If you are in a sticky situation, don't hesitate to use whatever you have in your hand to defend yourself.
- If you feel you are being followed regularly or stalked, do not hesitate to report to someone as it could become dangerous.
- Beware of unsafe neighborhoods.

Your Body Your Rule

POCSO Act - Legal support:

So how do you get justice for child sexual abuse? Did you know that the Indian government has enacted POCSO (Protection of Children against Sexual Offences Act) in 2012?

This Act puts the burden of proof on the accused rather than the child. The accused has to prove that he/she is innocent instead of the child proving that the crime took place.

Procedure with POCSO:

This Act provides the child with friendly statement recording, medical examinations, and examination of the child in court.

- Child-friendly courts are now mandatory in each district.
- The child will be accompanied by a parent, legal guardian or someone he/she trusts, during the hearing in court.
- The child will not be facing the accused at any time during the procedure.

The POCSO offers further compensations to the child for immediate relief or rehabilitation and if the child is in need of care and protection, arrangements are made at once.

VIII
Conclusion

Here we are, at the end of our session! Hope you kids learned lots of new and educational stuff.

Child abuse has become common in our society nowadays despite educating countless number of adults about it. It is only you who can act in the situation and find a means of stopping it from happening. And always remember to be on your guard for any situation. This will help you be aware of anything throughout your lifetime. Take care of your body and develop a healthy sense of respect towards your body. Seek any information you require from trusted sources. Your thoughtful approach to your body will help you develop a healthy sexuality. With whatever you have learnt here, you will be able to identify any dangerous situations and act accordingly. You will also be able to help yourself and any of your friend who might have been or continue to being abused by an elder with your presence of mind.

A Word About Wording_Glossary

This Glossary is intended to assist kids in understanding the terms in sex education. All language is constantly evolving; new terms are introduced, while others fade from use or change their meaning over time. This remains true for the terms and definitions included in this Glossary.

Agender: A person who does not identify with any gender.

AIDS (Acquired Immune Deficiency Syndrome): AIDS is caused by the human immunodeficiency virus (HIV) and may occur if HIV is untreated. People do not die from AIDS but from an infection their body acquires as a result of their weakened immune system.

Asexual: A person who does not experience sexual attraction but may experience other forms of attraction (e.g., intellectual and/or emotional).

Bisexual: A person who is emotionally, romantically, and/or sexually attracted to more than one gender, though not necessarily simultaneously, in the same way, or to the same degree.

Bullying: Physically, mentally, and/or emotionally intimidating and/or harming an individual or members of a group.

Comprehensive Sex Education/Comprehensive Sexuality Education: Programs that build a foundation of knowledge and skills relating to human development, relationships, decisionmaking, abstinence, contraception, and disease prevention.

Consent: Informed, voluntary, and mutual agreement between people to engage in an activity.

External Condoms: A sheath of latex or polyurethane that is worn on the penis to reduce the risk of pregnancy, and/or sexually transmitted diseases (STDs) when one is engaging in sexual behavior. External condoms are also called male condoms.

Gay: An umbrella term used for people who are romantically, emotionally, and/or sexually attracted to people of the same gender.

Gender Binary: A socially constructed system of viewing gender as consisting solely of two categories - male and female—in which no other possibilities for gender are believed to exist.

Gender Identity: It may include male, female, agender, androgynous, genderqueer, nonbinary, transgender, and many others, or a combination thereof.

Harassment: Unwelcome or offensive behavior by one person to another that can be sexual or nonsexual in nature.

Lesbian: A person who identifies as a woman who is romantically, emotionally, and/or sexually attracted to other women.

Masturbation: Touching one's own body for sexual pleasure. This may include stimulation of one's own genitals and commonly results in orgasm.

Puberty: A stage of human biological development during which adolescents become sexually mature and capable of reproduction. Physical changes may include hair growth around the genitals, menstruation, sperm production, breast growth, and much more.

Rape: A type of sexual assault that involves vaginal, anal, or oral sex using a body part or an object without consent. Rape is a form of sexual assault, but not all sexual assault is rape.

Sex Trafficking: The recruitment, transportation, transfer, harboring, provision, or obtaining of an individual who under threat, force, coercion, fraud, deception, or abuse of power is sexually exploited for the financial gain of another.

Sexual Abuse: Any sort of unwanted sexual contact, including but not limited to, force, threats, or taking advantage of an individual, often over a period of time. A single act of sexual abuse is usually referred to as a "sexual assault."

Sexual Harassment: Unwelcome sexual advances, requests for sexual favors, and other unwanted verbal or physical conduct of a sexual nature.

Sexual Intercourse: It may mean different things to different people, but could include behaviors such as vaginal sex, oral sex, or anal sex.

Sexuality: Sexuality describes how one experiences and expresses one's self as a sexual being.

Sexually Transmitted Diseases (STDs): Common infections caused by bacteria, viruses, or parasites that are transmitted from one person who has the infection to another during sexual contact that involves exchange of fluids or skin-to-skin contact.

Transgender: A person whose gender identity and/or expression is not aligned with the sex they were assigned at birth.

Trusted Adult: A person to whom a student can turn to in a time of need who can offer support and guidance.